The Beginners Guide to Breyer® Model Horse Showing

(Halter classes)

Bonnie Valentine

ISBN: 978-0989358910

A very special thanks to Lucy Kusluch and Kelly Diller for editing and input.

Table of Contents

Preface

As someone who has been in the model horse hobby since 1976 I can tell you that "back in the day" hobbyists had to learn everything the hard way. The only guides were other people in the hobby, thankfully most will gladly help. That still does not assist with the fifty questions that most people forget to ask at the appropriate time. My first reference book *The Beginners Guide to Breyer® Collecting* has helped many starting out in the hobby find a path through all the chat rooms, auction sites, and chaos of Breyerfest®. The concept of showing model horses is foreign to those who never heard of it, and even some who are involved in the hobby have trouble explaining it to someone else. So here it is, the solution, at least the first part, halter classes. A book on performance showing will follow as that is a topic that merits a manual all to itself.

Chapter One – What is a Model Horse Show and Where Do I Start?

A model horse show is a very perplexing matter until it is explained. Just how does one show a model horse; it's just plastic? It is not as absurd as it sounds. Actually, it can be addicting. The show holder or host (person or group putting on the show) will typically rent a church hall, fire hall, or other venue that has the space to accommodate a lot of tables and model horses.

Then they will choose a date, put together a list of classes (class list), rules, and entry procedures, as well as other relevant information such as area hotels, directions, and will there be food at the show or are there nearby restaurants?

The show holder will also have to decide if their event is going to be a NAN (North American Nationals) qualifier or just a regular show. In both cases the class list and entry packet must be made available to potential showers. Normally the information is on a website or Facebook page, only a few still do things via US mail.

Once all the information is available, showers will access it and start sending in entries along with the appropriate entry fee. Some shows want a list of the horses you are bringing, others do not require one. Traditionally most shows only allow fifty horses per shower or charge an additional entry fee when that number is surpassed. Base entry fees average forty dollars and up. Considering the cost of hall rental, NAN cards, and awards, most show holders are lucky to break even.

Participants bring up their model horses and place them on the table, also called the show ring, to be judged according to the class standards. Well, it's not quite that simple but fear not, all related topics will be covered in detail throughout this book.

A fire department social hall used to host a show.

Chapter Two – Showing a Model Horse in Original Finish Plastic Halter Classes

At a model horse show the <u>original finish plastic</u> (OF (pronounced oh-eff) from this point forward) halter division is often the largest and the easiest to participate in. OF models are those that have not been altered in any way, shape, or form and are just as it arrived from the factory when it was brand new. Older models may have some scratches or other flaws that will be covered later in the book.

Requirements

The only requirement to show an original finish plastic model is just that, an original finish plastic model horse.

Choosing a Model Horse

A model horse's condition is by far the most important criteria. Unless it is a very old and rare piece, the model must be free of scratches, dents, overspray, rubs, yellowing, and any other flaws. Look closely for any hoof or ear tip rubs as they will cost placing in the show ring. Models that meet show criteria are referred to as "live show quality" and are difficult to find as many manufacturers make plastic model horses primarily for the toy market.

A few OF Breyers in a collectability class

China collectability entries

Chapter Three - Categories: Breed and Collectability

Some shows offer both breed and collectability halter competition. It is not uncommon for models to be judged under both categories simultaneously; also referred to as double judged. Collectability entries are only judged on rarity, condition, and desirability. Judges will inspect and place the model appropriately in one or both categories. It is possible for a model to prevail in both breed and collectability, however it is rare, most fit in one category or the other best.

Breed entries are also judged on condition and how well the model meets the breed standard of what type of horse the exhibitor has labeled the model as. Shows require participants to assign a breed and gender to each model that will be exhibited. Choosing a breed or gender is not as simple as looking at what the manufacturer's package says. The box might say "Arabian Stallion" when the horse inside better resembles a "Quarter Horse Mare." Research is the key. Horse breed reference books are the best resource as well as online materials. Many public libraries carry horse breed books. Keep in mind that selecting rare, obscure, or extinct breeds will make it necessary to provide documentation with the show entry. The documentation can be as simple as a hand written description on an index card to a color copy from a breed book nicely laminated or in a sheet protector. Just remember to keep it short and to the point as the judge will be looking at a lot of models and does not have time to read a multi-page thesis on every breed.

Gender is obvious on some model horses while others it is difficult to tell by looking. If the model is refined appearing then it should be a mare. More muscular or larger models should be stallions or geldings. In the case of a stallion if the parts are there then that is what the model should be shown as.

Veteran showers are always more than happy to assist others with breed assignments as well as explaining why a certain horse has conformation that suits one breed better than another.

The chart that follows is a very valuable reference for breed assignment of various molds of Breyer horses. It is just a guide and not a breed assignment bible. Factors such as color may change breed assignment. For example, an Arabian with Appaloosa markings cannot show as a pure Arabian. It would go in a part Arabian or Grade/Mix class. Grade is a term used to refer to a horse of unknown breeding just as a dog is called a mutt if breeding is mixed or unknown.

Breyer Molds and Breed Assignment Suggestions

Mold	Breed Suggestions
Action Stock Horse Foal*	Grade/mix
Adios	older Standardbred, foundation-bred QH, other stock, grade or cross, light draft cross, Spanish Norman, Irish Draught
Alborozo	Andalusian
Amber	Morgan, pinto, appaloosa
American Saddlebred	Saddlebred, national show horse
Andalusian Stallion	Andalusian, Lusitano
Appaloosa Performance Horse	Foundation Appaloosa
Ashley	Any light or sport breed
Ashquar	Arabian, part Arabian
Balking Mule	mule
Belgian	Draft, draft cross
Big Ben	Dutch Warmblood, Hanoverian, Oldenburg
Black Beauty*	Heavy warmblood breeds
Black Stallion*	Arabian, Hispano Arab
Bluegrass Bandit	Tennessee Walking Horse
Boyla	Akhal-Teke
Bouncer	Welsh Pony, mix
Brighty (donkey)*	donkey
Brown Sunshine (mule)	Mule
Buckshot*	Does not show well

Carrick	TB, TB cross
Cantering Welsh Pony	Grade, mixed breed pony
Cigar	TB, TB Cross, Appendix QH
Cleveland Bay	Cleveland Bay, part breed Draft/TB, Irish Draft
Clydesdale Foal	Clydesdale, other draft
Clydesdale Mare	Clydesdale, other draft
Clydesdale Stallion	Clydesdale, other draft
Cody*	Does not show well
Criollo	Criollo, – Other Iberian Breeds
Donkey	donkey
El Pastor	Paso Fino, Rocky Mountain Horse
Esprit	Morab
Ethereal	Choctaw, part arab
Family Arabian Foal*	Arabian, Shagya
Family Arabian Mare*	Arabian, Shagya
Family Arabian Stallion*	Arabian, part-Arabian, Shagya, Quarab, Morab
Fighting Stallion*	Grade, mustang
Five Gaiter	Saddlebred
Fjord	Fjord
Flash	American Sport Pony
Foundation Stallion	Azteca, Spanish Barb, Andalusian, Lusitano, Mustang
Friesian	Friesian, Friesian cross, Finnhorse, draft-cross, Cleveland Bay cross

Fury Prancer*	Best for collectability only
Galiceno	Galiceno, Criollo
Gem Twist	Belgian WB, Dutch WB, Danish WB
Gilen	Swedish Warmblood, Holsteiner, Mecklenberger
Giselle	Swedish Warmblood, Holsteiner, Mecklenberger
Goffert	Friesian
Grazing Foal*	Most light breeds
Grazing Mare*	QH, TB, Standardbred
Gypsy Vanner	Gypsy Vanner
Hackney	Hackney
Haflinger	Haflinger
Halla	Standardbred, Akhal-Teke, TB cross, American Warmblood
Hanoverian	Hanoverian, Oldenburger, Holsteiner, Westphalian, Dutch WB
Huckleberry Bey	Arabian, part-Arabian
Iberian	Andalusian
Icelandic	Icelandic Horse
Ideal Quarter Horse*	Does not show well
Idocus	Dutch WB
In-Between Mare* (RARE)	Best for collectability only Part Arabian
Indian Pony	Mustang, grade, foundation Appaloosa

John Henry	TB, TB cross, Standardbred, MFT
Jumping Horse*	Hanoverian
Justin Morgan	Old style Morgan, MFT
Kennebec Count	Morab
Khemosabi*	Grade, does not show well as any breed
Kipper*	Collectability only
Lady Phase	QH, American stock breeds
Lady Roxanna*	Arabian, Arabian cross, Shagya
Latigo	Stock breeds
Le Fire	Part arabian
Legionario III	Andalusian, Lusitano
Llanarth True Briton*	Does not show well
Lonesome Glory	TB, TB-cross, Akhal-Teke/QH, Akhal-Teke /TB
Lying Down Foal*	Does not show well
Make a Wish	Arabian, Part arabian
Man O'War	Thoroughbred
Marabella	Morgan, Paso Fino, MFT
Marwari	Marwari
Midnight Sun*	Does not show well, TWH
Midnight Tango	Miniature Horse
Missouri Fox Trotter	Missouri Fox Trotter
Misty	grade pony, Chincoteage pony
Misty's Twilight*	Does not show well
Morgan	Morgan
Morganglanz	Trakehner, Swedish WB

Mustang (semi-rearing)	Mustang, Grade, mixed stock breed
Newsworthy	Welsh Pony Section B
Nokota	Mustang
Nursing Foal	Any light breed
Old Timer*	Grade, mixed breed
Pacer*	Standardbred pacer
Peruvian Paso Stallion	Peruvian Paso
Phantom Wings*	Light pony breeds
Phar Lap	Does not show well, American mustang
Pluto	Lipizzaner, other Spanish
Pony of the Americans (POA)	POA, Quarter Pony
Proud Arabian Foal	Any light breed
Proud Arabian Mare*	Polish Arabian
Proud Arabian Stallion*	Polish Arabian
Quarter Horse Gelding	Foundation QH, draft cross
Race Horse*	Collectability only
Rain*	Collectability only
Rejoice	ASB, NSH
Roemer	Dutch WB
Roxy*	Does not show well
Roy	Draft cross
Ruffian	TB
Rugged Lark*	Grade, does not show well as any breed
Running Foal*	Almost any light breed
Running Mare*	Morgan, Morab, grade, Shagya

Running Stallion*	Grade
Saddlebred Weanling	Saddlebred
Salinero	WB, sporthorse
San Domingo	Mustang, grade
Scratching Foal	Any light breed
Sea Star	Any light breed
Secretariat	TB
Sham	Arabian, Arabian-cross
Sherman Morgan*	Does not show well
Shetland Pony	British Shetland, grade pony
Shire	Shire
Show Jumping Warmblood	WB, British sporthorse breeds, Aussie Stock Horse
Silver	Grade, TB, TB cross
Smart Chic Olena	QH
Smarty Jones	TB, racing bred QH
Smoky*	Grade, mustang
Spirit*	Does not show well
Stock Horse Foal	Almost any stock breed
Stock Horse Mare*	Does not show well, Appendix QH
Stock Horse Stallion*	Does not show well, QH
Stormy	Almost any pony breed
Strapless	TB, TB cross, American WB
Stud Spider	Most stock breeds
Susecion	Part arabian
Thoroughbred Mare	TB, TB cross
Totilas	Dutch WB

Touch of Class	TB, Selle Francais
Trakehner	WB
Weather Girl	Arabian, Part arabian
Western Horse*	Grade
Western Pony*	Grade
Western Prancing Horse*	Grade
Wyatt	Stock breed
Wintersong	Various draft with heavy feathering according to color of model
Wixom	Any draft breed without feathering
Zebra	zebra
Zippo Pine Bar	QH, other stock

* As a general rule this mold does not show well in breed due to design flaws or lack of detail. Collectability is an entirely different matter.

ASB= American Saddlebred
MFT= Missouri Fox trotter
POA= Pony of the Americans
QH= Quarter Horse
TB= Thoroughbred
WB= Warmblood

General Breed Notes:

<u>MAKE SURE THE COAT COLOR IS BREED APPROPRIATE!</u> **Horses come in many colors, the same mold painted as a bay would be assigned a different breed than one with appaloosa markings. Check real horse coat colors. Breeds on the chart are suggestions only, a model may be a color that is not appropriate for the normal breed assignment.**

In addition to the previous chart pay attention to the following breed assignment rules. These are the ones that are most commonly missed by new showers:

Andalusian: only come in the following colors grey, black, or bay. The registry just recently accepted other colors so show documentation until this change is well known. The safe approach is still to show model as a Lusitano if it is any solid color other than bay, black, or grey.

Friesian: classified as a carriage breed not a draft.

Warmbloods: some must have a brand, make sure if the model does if it is a breed requirement for what it is being shown as.

Welsh Ponies: Section A sturdy not to exceed 12 hands tall, Section B riding pony not to exceed 13.2 hands tall.

Paint/ Pinto: A Paint is a breed of horse, a pinto is a coat pattern.

Unrealistic Colors: Models that come in colors that do not exist such as blue and gold are classified under the unrealistic colors classes.

Chapter Four – The Class list

The class list is the order of events, or the literary for the day of the show.

Here is an example of the OF plastic light breeds division at a show where classes are judged for both breed and collectability at the same time.

1. Open Hartland (*class for Hartland models*)
2. Stone Arabian (*this show separates Breyer and Peter Stone models, not all shows do so.*
3. Breyer Arabian
4. Stone Part Arabian
5. Breyer Part Arabian
6. Stone Morgan/Morab
7. Breyer Morgan/Morab (*after this class any model that won a 1st or 2nd place would be called back for light breed championship. In this case it would be both breed and collectability.*

Champion/Reserve light Breed
Champion/Reserve light Breed Collectability

It is at the discretion of the show holder as to how classes are divided. Some are split by manufacturer, others combine them all together. Classes may also be split by scale with a separate division for Stablemates®. This is all up to the show holders to determine. Obviously some things never show together such as original finish and custom pieces.

Chapter Five – Tagging and documenting

Models must be able to be identified at the show for recordkeeping or if something gets misplaced. Almost all shows require a hang tag with breed and gender on one side and the horse's name and owner's initials on the other side. The reason for hiding the initials is that during judging, the identity of the owner of the model should not be known as this could skew the results.

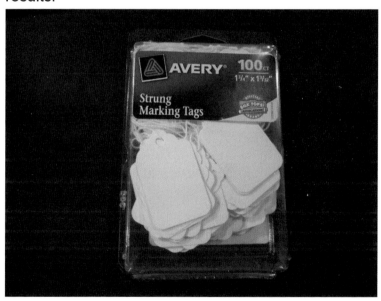

Example of string tags. Any size is fine as long as there is ample space to write all the required information.

Side of tag that faces up with breed and gender of horse. It is acceptable to hand write the tags as long as it is legible.

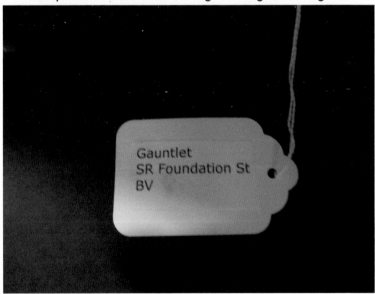

Other side that the judge will turn up after placing class to record results. Must at least have name of horse and owner's initials. This tag also lists what model it is; that is optional and can help with organization.

Rare breeds will require additional information. Some showers leave a breed book open on the table, while others photocopy the page, and still some even make elaborate cards and such to go along with their setups. Always be brief and to the point, the judges do not have time to read a long elaborate history.

Collectability classes require a little extra as far as documentation. Never assume a judge is familiar with the item. Always have a card (or original certificate if available) stating the years of production, quantity produced (if applicable), and any other information such as chalky version, one sock version, and so on.

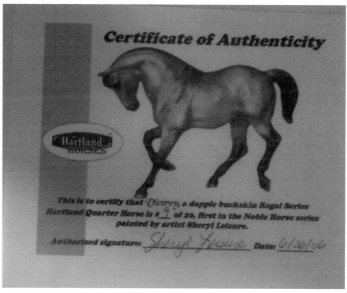

A certificate of authenticity proves this Hartland is #9 of 20 models produced.

Chapter Six – NAMHSA / NAN Cards

NAMHSA – North American Model Horse Showers Association (www.namhsa.org) is the organization that oversees sanctioned model horse showing and hosts the national championships once a year. Established in 1994 the first National Championship was held in Lexington, Kentucky in 1995 and is still held there every other year. Visit the website for a list of sanctioned shows in your area.

The United States is split into eleven regions for NAN (North American Nationals) with a representative overseeing each region. All NAMHSA officers and representatives are elected by the members.

NAN cards are one of the holy grails of model horse showing. How do you get them? Just compete at a NAMHSA approved show and place first or second in a class that is NAN eligible. First and second place winners get a card that can be sent in at a later date with an entry fee to participate at the nationals. Cards are currently valid for 4 years.

As part of the Merit Awards Program, cards can also be submitted for awards plaques or certificates once any of the following titles have been earned.

Superior Event Horse (SEH)
Superior Halter Horse (SHH)
Versatility Award (VA)
Performance Versatility (PV) Awards
Halter Legacy Award (HLA)
Performance Legacy Award (PLA)
Halter Hall of Champions Award (HHCA)
Performance Hall of Champions Award (PHCA)
Versatility Hall of Champions Award (VHCA)
Division Horse Hall of Champions Award (DHHCA)
Supreme Halter Hall of Fame Award (SHHFA)
Supreme Performance Hall of Fame Award (SPHFA)
Supreme Versatility Award (SVA)
Supreme Performance Versatility Award (SPVA).

Refer to the NAMHSA website for the criteria for each title. A fee is required to receive a merit award to cover the cost of it.

NAN cards come in three colors. Green is for breed classes, pink is for performance, and yellow is for non-breed which is normally collectability or workmanship.

NON-BREED HALTER

NAMHSA

60/res 9

Southwest PA Classic 10th annual year of the horse show
9/27/2014
This ticket qualifies for the following NAN shows:
2015 / 2016 / 2017 / 2018

IMPORTANT:

To enter this horse in the North American Nationals (NAN) show in any of the years printed on the label above, you must request a NAN Entry Packet. For the most current information on NAN Entry and deadlines, and all the information on NAMHSA in general, go to the NAMHSA website at www.namhsa.org or contact the NAMHSA secretary. DO NOT DUPLICATE THIS CARD.

NAMHSA
North American Model Horse Shows Association

North American Nationals™ (NAN)
Official Qualification Ticket

Class Name:

_____

Horse Name:

_____

Owner Name:

_____

The above information must be filled out by the winner of this ticket. Do this IMMEDIATELY. This is your ONLY proof of winning this qualification; it can not be replaced if lost, duplicated or not filled out. **DO NOT DUPLICATE THIS CARD.** Only this actual ticket can be presented for NAN entry or NAMHSA Merit Awards.

If you sell the horse that won this qualification, you must send this actual ticket to the new owner. New owner: write your name on the BACK of this ticket. Do NOT cross out ANY information written above.

HALTER

Southwest PA Classic 10th annual year of the horse show

9/27/2014

This ticket qualifies for the following NAN shows:
2015 / 2016 / 2017 / 2018

IMPORTANT:

To enter this horse in the North American Nationals (NAN) show in any of the years printed on the label above, you must request a NAN Entry Packet. For the most current information on NAN Entry and deadlines, and all the information on NAMHSA in general, go to the NAMHSA website at www.namhsa.org or contact the NAMHSA secretary. DO NOT DUPLICATE THIS CARD.

NAMHSA

NON-BREED HALTER

Southwest PA Classic 10th annual year of the horse show

9/27/2014

This ticket qualifies for the following NAN shows:
2015 / 2016 / 2017 / 2018

IMPORTANT:

To enter this horse in the North American Nationals (NAN) show in any of the years printed on the label above, you must request a NAN Entry Packet. For the most current information on NAN Entry and deadlines, and all the information on NAMHSA in general, go to the NAMHSA website at www.namhsa.org or contact the NAMHSA secretary. DO NOT DUPLICATE THIS CARD.

NAMHSA

PERFORMANCE

Southwest PA Classic 10th annual year of the horse show

9/27/2014

This ticket qualifies for the following NAN shows:
2015 / 2016 / 2017 / 2018

IMPORTANT:

To enter this horse in the North American Nationals (NAN) show in any of the years printed on the label above, you must request a NAN Entry Packet. For the most current information on NAN Entry and deadlines, and all the information on NAMHSA in general, go to the NAMHSA website at www.namhsa.org or contact the NAMHSA secretary. DO NOT DUPLICATE THIS CARD.

NAMHSA

Chapter Seven – Other Important Details

Keep it Clean

Model horses competing in halter must be clean. Absolutely no dust, dirt, or other debris can be anywhere on the model. Do not use cleaners that will add a coat or film to the model as the result may be disqualification. Use a soft damp cloth for larger areas and a makeup brush for smaller details. At home it is fine to use a mild soap and water to remove dust from difficult to clean areas. Keep several makeup or paint brushes in with your show models for last minute touch-ups.

Equipment

Absolutely no props or tack are required to show in OF plastic. Halters may or may not be permitted as per the rules of each individual show. Do not use a halter unless absolutely certain on how to properly put it on the model. Judges generally do not give entries extra credit for halters. The only exception is if a collectability piece originally came with an accessory.

Entry limits

The number of models allowed in each class is typically limited to three. Most shows offer a variety of halter classes allowing the shower to bring plenty of models as well as have an opportunity to showcase favorite pieces from any collection. A few shows allow additional entries on a cost per additional model basis. Try not to show too many models at first as it will become frustrating trying to keep up with everything. A fun day will quickly turn into a hectic, confusing, and chaotic mess.

Awards

Awards can be anything. Real custom printed flat ribbons and rosettes, medallions, engraved plates, homemade paper ribbons, trophies (bought or made), models, etc. There are more options for awards then anyone can imagine. Each show is different. Remember the more expensive the awards the higher the entry fee unless items are donated.

What are the Judges Doing?

The model horse show judge (sometimes distinguished by a badge; almost always has a clipboard) has the distinct honor and privilege of trying to decide which horse on the table is the best example for the criteria of the class. This can be a daunting task since in many cases there might be twelve of the exact same model exhibited in a single class.

Mentor

Prior to a show if you are new ask the show holder if they could assign you a mentor (an experienced and trusted advisor) to help walk you through the show. They will offer advice and specific pointers that will help you to learn all about showing halter.

Proxy Showing

Proxy showing is when a person brings models that belong to someone else and shows them for the owner. Typical costs are $1.00 per horse per class with a limit on the number of models that can be entered. This is something that you do not want to attempt until you have some experience showing as it is hard enough to show your own models in the beginning.

Naming Models

Unless you want the show judge to be your worst enemy keep the names of your models short and sweet. For example, no judge wants to write down "Heza Storm Chasing Hasenpfeffer Kinda Guy". If you must have this please just use H.S.C.H.K.G. on the tags. There is nothing wrong with names like Joe, Sally, Cocoa, etc. Judges just want to quickly record results; not write a novel of long horse names.

Online Forums

The internet is a fantastic resource for model horse showing information. There are Yahoo® groups, Facebook® pages, and blogs dedicated entirely to the topic of showing model horses.

Show Etiquette

- NEVER, EVER move a horse in the show ring to place yours on the table. Ask someone what to do if there is not enough space for your horse.

- Do not bother the judge while a class is being evaluated.

- Do not pick up anything that does not belong to you without permission.

- No running, yelling, loud noises in the show hall.

- Pets are not permitted, service animals are of course allowed.

- All decisions of the judges are final. Do not cause a scene if you do not agree with class placements.

- Silence your cell phone.

- Pay attention to what is going on, it is rude to delay the show for everyone else.

- Have fun, if it is not enjoyable why are you doing it?

Chapter Eight – Packing for a Show

There are as many different ways to pack for a models horse show as there are types of containers to put them in. Some showers use plastic bins, others have a hard metal case with a foam lining for each piece, and once in a while someone shows up with a cardboard box.

Plastic bins are the most economical long term solution

Metal cases are very effective but can get expensive

Wrapping the models

Bubble wrap, towels, pony pouches, old t-shirts, some use puppy training pads; what to encase a model horse in to protect it from damage?

Pony pouches are cloth cases horse designed to accommodate various sized models. Look up the term on the internet and you will find several sources to purchase them or instructions to make your own.

Bubble wrap works well but uses a lot of space. Towels and old shirts do the job. Very valuable models should always be wrapped to survive a hundred foot drop just in case.

Newspaper is not recommended as the print rubs off on everything. Not good to open your show string of horses only to discover all the whites are now gray or have the imprint of the Sunday comics on them. The choice of what to use is a matter of personal preference.

Moving Around

A small investment in a hand truck or dolly to move around the totes is well worth it. Even a folding version can tote several bins at once. Some rope or a few tie straps are a good idea as they will secure the load.

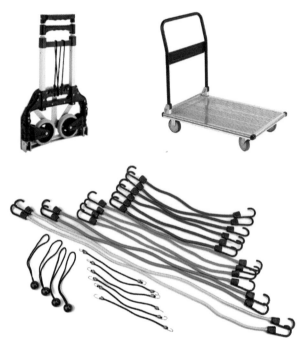

Two different types of handcarts and bungee cords

The Order of Things and Unpacking

Heed this advice when packing for a show. Check the class list and see what your first classes of the day are. Pack all the models you will need for the first few hours of the show together. Use more than one container if necessary and label it. That way you will have the models you need initially ready to unpack first thing. This can be a show saver if you run late or find that there is not enough room to get all your models out at one time. Missed classes are not recalled, there is only one chance to participate.

Unpacking will be much easier if the above advice is followed. Another issue that arises is setting the horses on your table so they do not fall. Some show participants take their chances, others use upright dish racks or pegs in a board. A tablecloth is optional, if used make sure it is not too long and gets caught on something spilling your models to the floor. The fancier the setup the more time it takes to get ready. Keep it as simple as possible in the beginning.

A nice display of models with pegs to prevent tipping over

An adjustable pot lid rack or a plastic coated plate organizer rack
are great to prevent models from falling.

Chapter Nine – Custom Models

Custom models are anything that has been repainted, re-sculpted, or an original resin piece painted by the artist or anyone else. Showing custom models is fiercely competitive and often times requires a major investment unless you are able to paint your own pieces.

Models in any custom division can be judged for breed and workmanship. It is up to the individual shows if one or both are on the class list. Workmanship is an evaluation of the preparatory and finish work.

Some common categories are:

- Custom Breed
- Custom Workmanship
- Artist resin
- China/ Resin
- Custom by owner
- Custom by other

Any of these can be combined to be double judged for breed and workmanship at the same time.

Custom model by Towns End Art owned by Donna Looman

Another custom model by Towns End Art

Chapter Ten - Show Day Walkthrough

This chapter will cover what occurs at a normal day at a model horse show. Let's just say that the show starts at 9 am and it is a one hour drive. The show hall opens at 8 am so you will need to leave no later than 6:45 am (even earlier if you like to allow additional extra time). At this point your entry should have been long sent in and all your models should be packed, tagged, and loaded in the vehicle ready for morning departure. You should also bring drinks, meals, or snacks that you need for the day if you do not wish to buy these items or the show is not providing them. Being a copy of the class list and make sure you have directions to the show and a contact number in case you have trouble finding it.

After arrival at the venue walk in and see if you are assigned a table or get to pick your own. Check in if required and pick up any packets or paperwork the show holder has (if any). Bring in your first bin or two of horses that needs to be unpacked for earliest classes. Find your mentor if you arranged for one and introduce yourself if they do not find you first. Continue unpacking, take your time - it will be a long day. Make sure anyone who comes with you and is not showing brings something to do or has plans to go do something else. Boredom is no fun!

At this point there may be several announcements, pay attention. Someone will announce it is time to start setting up the first classes in the various rings. When your first class is called bring up any entries. Check model for last minute dust/debris, verify the tag is the correct way, and any needed documentation is present. Once the judge closes the class do not touch anything on the table until judging is complete. After the class is judged promptly pick up models and any awards. If any models are done showing for the day it is fine to pack them away. Place any horse that has won a first or second place aside for callbacks.

Several divisions may be running at the same time. That is why it is imperative not to try to show too many models when starting out. Keep alert. When a division is done and call backs are announced bring up anything that has won a first or second place with NAN cards and awards. Some shows only call back first place winners - it is at the discretion of the show holder and/or judges to decide. If you are lucky enough to get a grand or reserve championship, keep those models out until the end of the day if there is going to be an overall championship.

There may or may not be an official lunch break. Especially if the show serves food at the hall, rather than stop the show completely judges may alternate lunch breaks. Someone may also fill in while the judge takes a break to keep the show moving along.

Throughout the day there could be raffles, silent auctions, contests, and fun classes. Different shows have different events. None of these things are required.

Once you have finished showing for the day carefully pack everything back up and head for home. Hopefully the day has been a pleasant one and you have discovered another aspect of the model horse hobby.

Printed in Great Britain
by Amazon